"Tell Them I Love Them"

"Tell Them
I Love Them"

by
Joyce Meyer

Harrison House
Tulsa, Oklahoma

4th Printing
Over 75,000 in Print

Tell Them I Love Them
ISBN 0-89274-783-8
Copyright © 1995 by Joyce Meyer
Life In The Word, Inc.
P.O. Box 655
Fenton, Missouri 63026

Published by Harrison House, Inc.
P.O. Box 35035
Tulsa, Oklahoma 74153

Contents

Introduction

I believe that what people need more than anything is a revelation of God's love for them personally. I believe this to be the foundation upon which victorious living as a Christian must stand. We do not need head knowledge concerning God's love; we need a revelation. This can only be given by the Holy Spirit and will be given as each believer meditates upon the love of God, observes the love of God in his own life and seeks that revelation through the written Word of God and also through prayer.

It is fairly easy to accept that God loves the whole world enough to send Jesus to die for the world. But it is a little more difficult to believe that if you had been the only person on the face of the earth, that God loves *you* so much that He would have sent Jesus to die for *you* and *you* alone.

After many years of being a frustrated Christian, I came to understand God's love.

God graciously revealed to me, through the Holy Spirit, His love for me personally. That single revelation has changed my entire life and my walk with Him.

I believe that what you read in this book will bring you new insight and understanding concerning the love of God. I believe it will place a new hunger in you to have this revelation for your very own. I exhort you to read the book slowly, to use it as a study aid and to meditate upon the Scriptures and the thoughts that you will find contained in the pages that follow.

This book is submitted to you in humility, knowing that I am nothing apart from Him and that whatever revelation and understanding I have of His Word, it is only by His grace.

1

····························

God Loves You!

"For God so loved the world, that he gave his only begotten Son, that whosoever believeth in him should not perish, but have everlasting life."

John 3:16

God wants a family, so God made us to be His kids. He does not want us to act like babies, but He wants us to act like His kids. He wants us to depend on Him, rely on Him, lean on Him, love Him and *let Him love us*. He wants us to trust Him and to reach out to Him when we have a need. He wants to have a personal relationship with *you*.

Most of us take John 3:16 in too broad a scope. "Oh, yes, I know Jesus died for the world," but we are *not* just a group of general people down here that Jesus died for. He died for each one of us. *He died for you!*

If *you* had been the only person on the face of this earth, He would have died just for *you*. He would have gone through all the suffering for *you*. He died for *you*! God loves you so much. He loves you with an everlasting love.

One day I was driving down the road, and God spoke to my heart and said, "Joyce, you're the apple of My eye." I didn't even know that Scripture was in the Bible. The devil came in with a thought right behind that and said, "Well, isn't that a bunch of pride? Who do you think you are?" And so I thought to myself, "Oh, I shouldn't be thinking like that." It goes against our carnal thinking to realize that we *are* special, that we are gifted, that we are different. Each one of us is an individual, created by our Father to be different from the person next to us.

As I was thinking about it, God showed me a little mental picture of a lady standing in a supermarket by a large pile of apples. She looked all around and found one that was really super then reached in to get the very best one. What God was saying to me was that I was the best apple to Him. I was the special one. That doesn't seem right, but you see, God says that to every one of us. It isn't that He is saying that you are really someone neat, and everyone else is no good. He is saying that we are all special. It is in the Word, and the Word is for every one of us. *You are the apple of God's eye.*

I didn't receive what God had said to me because I felt condemned thinking such nice things about myself. About two days later I opened my Bible to Psalm 17:8, and there it was staring me in the face: "Keep me as the apple of the eye, hide me under the shadow of thy wings." I said, "Oops, that was really God. I *am* the apple of God's eye." For the longest time, I felt so special every time I thought about it.

People have a craving, and a longing, and a desire in their hearts to be loved. God made us that way. Many people believe that God loves the world and that He loves Jesus, but they have a hard time believing that God loves them. Yet the Word teaches that God loves them as much as He loves Jesus. He loves *you* as much as He loves Jesus. Let's look at John 5:20:

"For the Father loveth the Son, and sheweth him all things that himself doeth: and he will shew him greater works than these, that ye may marvel."

God says here, "I'm doing all these great things through Jesus, and greater things than this through Jesus, that *you* may marvel" (author's paraphrase). Do you know that it is fine to marvel at something, to be in awe of what God is doing?

We read these Scriptures, but we often miss what God wants to do for us. He wants us to look at the great works He did through Jesus and just marvel and say, "Boy, God, that's wonderful what You did through Jesus." Then He wants you to turn in the Bible to John 14:12 where Jesus says: "He that believeth on me, the works that I do shall he do also; and greater works than these shall he do; because I go unto my Father."

God will do the same things through you, and greater works than these shall you do because Jesus went to His father. Do you believe that? Do you really believe that God loves you and will use you?

The Lord ministered to me one day when I was studying and said, "Joyce, I do so many things for people every day because I love them, and they don't ever see it. They don't recognize it at all. I'll give you just one example. Every day when I speak to the sun and say 'Rise,' I did it for Joyce, for Betty, for Jamie, for (fill in *your* name here)."

Stop and think about that. The sun rises in the sky every day for *you*. Yes, the sun! And we just take that for granted. We know the sun is going to come up every day, but it rises for *you*. When the rain comes in its season, it rains for *you*. When the snow comes, it comes for *you*. God loves you that much.

Deuteronomy 7:9 says,

"Know therefore that the Lord thy God, he is God, the faithful God, which keepeth covenant and mercy with them that love him and keep his commandments to a thousand generations."

Do you think that a thousand generations is long enough for you to get in on the love of God? You see, He is an everlasting God, and you can't wear God out. A lot of us think that we have just worn God out with our failures and messes, but you can't do that. Love can't be worn out, and you can't get God not to love you. Love is not something God does. It is Who He is.

Even the dirtiest, rottenest sinner that ever walked the face of this earth and would spit in the eyes of Jesus and say, "I want nothing to do with you; I'm perfectly satisfied to go to hell" – God loves him. So how could He not love those who have been chosen and set apart for God's purpose?

You may have already said, "I receive Jesus into my heart, and I love Him." But I ask you, *how much do you believe God loves you?*

This is a very simple message to you:

God loves you. But this is the basic foundation that God has to lay in you for you to understand everything else.

No matter what else you learn and how hard you study and seek the things of God, if you can't accept the fact that God loves you, you are not going to get very far. God's love for you is the foundation for your faith, for your freedom from sin and for your ability to step out in ministry to others without fear. *Will you receive His love for you?*

God loves *you*!

2

....

Am I Good Enough?

"Such hope never disappoints or deludes or shames us, for God's love has been poured out in our hearts through the Holy Spirit Who has been given to us.

"While we were yet in weakness [powerless to help ourselves], at the fitting time Christ died for (in behalf of) the ungodly.

"Now it is an extraordinary thing for one to give his life even for an upright man, though perhaps for a noble and lovable and generous benefactor someone might even dare to die.

"But God shows and clearly proves His [own] love for us by the fact that while we were still sinners, Christ (the Messiah, the Anointed One) died for us.

"Therefore, since we are now justified (acquitted, made righteous, and brought into right relationship with God) by Christ's blood, how much more [certain is it that] we shall be saved by Him from the indignation and wrath of God.

"For if while we were enemies we were reconciled to God through the death of His Son, it is much more [certain], now that we are reconciled, that we shall be saved (daily delivered from sin's dominion) through His [resurrection] life."

Romans 5:5-10 AMP

Many of us can believe that God loves us as long as we don't mess up. Most people don't like themselves very much, so they conclude that God can't be very impressed. Yet the Bible says, "What is man, that thou art mindful of him?" (Ps. 8:4). We are just simply God's creation, and *He loves us because He loves us*. He is love. (1 John 4:16.)

He loves you, and *you are special*. That means you are distinctive and unique. You are not supposed to be like me, and I am not supposed to be like you. And we will be miserable if we try to be like anyone else. All that does is give the devil an opportunity to tell you that you are not good enough. The thing is, with God, you don't have to be "good enough."

Did Jesus die for you because you were so great and wonderful, or did He die for you because He loved you? The Bible says that if He loved you enough to die for you, how much more then, being justified by His blood, does He now love you? (Rom. 5:8,9.) He loves you enough to cover your little daily mistakes. He loves you enough to get you through this day in power and victory.

God showed me an example one day of how He sees our mistakes and shortcomings. Imagine a little kid, about three or four years old, who is always watching mommy do her housework. She loves mommy so much that she gets a little bucket of water and a little rag and goes to the picture window on the front porch. She scrubs the window really well then gets a few paper towels and wipes the window.

Of course, it is all streaky and smeary and soapy. And when you see what she did, you realize she used your best cleaning rag, and you would like to wring her neck. But she comes in, and in her tiny sweet voice says, "Mommy, mommy, I washed your window. I did such a good job for you. I love you mommy."

A loving mother would say, "Oh, that's a wonderful thing you did. Thanks for helping." Then, as soon as the child was busy somewhere else, she would clean up the mess and give her some encouragement later not to do that again.

God told me that's what He does for us. He always cleans up our messes. If you are doing the best that you know how to do, that's all God expects from you. He doesn't expect you to do something you are not able to do. He can change you if you are willing to say, "You're right God, and I'm wrong. I've tried, and I can't change it." Then He will because He knows you can't make yourself better without His help.

"For since He Whom God has sent speaks the words of God [proclaims God's own message], God does not give Him His

Spirit sparingly or by measure, but boundless is the gift God makes of His Spirit!

"The Father loves the Son and has given (entrusted, committed) everything into His hand."

John 3:34,35 AMP

One day while I was studying, I was meditating on this verse and cried for joy when I realized that God doesn't give us His Spirit by measure. He doesn't give us just a little dab of this and a little dab of that.

Instead, He says, *"Here, take everything I've got."* Every bit of God's power and love are available to you today. He has all you need, and He wants you to receive it. Why? Because He loves you. You don't have to be good enough to deserve it because you couldn't do enough to deserve it anyway. You don't have to be pretty enough or smart enough. God wants to give to you because He loves you.

In Deuteronomy 7:6,7 AMP, God said,

"For you are a holy and set-apart people to the Lord your God; the Lord your

God has chosen you to be a special people to Himself out of all the peoples on the face of the earth.

"The Lord did not set His love upon you and choose you because you were more in number than any other people, for you were the fewest of all people."

God chose the Israelites to be His special people, and as the Church, we are the true spiritual Israel today. So this Scripture is for you just as much as for them. He said, "I didn't choose you because you were the largest tribe of people on the earth." Applied to us, that would say, "I didn't choose you because you did everything just right or because you were so wonderful."

He goes on to say that they were fewer than anyone else. As a matter of fact, if you are like me, you probably thought you were worse than anyone else before you got saved. Yet in verse 8 AMP, God says,

"But because the Lord loves you and because He would keep the oath which He had sworn to your fathers, the Lord has brought you out with a mighty hand and redeemed you out of the house of bondage, from the hand of Pharaoh king of Egypt."

That's shouting ground! God says, *"I set my love on you, and I told you you're holy. I told you you're special. I chose you, not because you're good and wonderful, but because I love you."* Do you know what God wants you to do today? He wants you to accept and receive His love.

For most of us, our biggest problem is that we don't like ourselves. We don't believe God loves us, or that anyone else loves us for that matter. We think, *How could they — I'm such a mess?* If you believe that you are nasty and ugly, then you are going to think, look and act nasty and ugly. You can't rise above the image of yourself that's in your heart.

My biggest problem used to be that I didn't like myself, and I spent at least 75 percent of my time trying to change myself. I thought I talked too much, so I tried to be quiet. But then if I was quiet, I would get depressed, and everyone would want to know why I was quiet. Then I would think, *But you told me I had a big mouth. Leave me alone. I'm just trying to be quiet.*

I can't tell you how many years I went through that. And still I was always getting into trouble with my mouth. A lot of people who are real talkers are married to partners who are real quiet. That just shows up your big mouth even more, and the devil will constantly remind you of it. And that's called *condemnation*.

God wants you to be free from condemnation, but it takes faith and boldness to be free. Do you know that no matter how guilty you feel it is not going to pay for one thing you did wrong? It is real tough to believe that God loves you when you have done something wrong.

The whole time the devil is beating on you and beating on you with thoughts about how bad and nasty and ugly you are. "You've done it now," he says. "Who do you think you are? God is never going to bless you, you dirty old thing, you. You couldn't witness to anybody now. You can't do anything right."

That's when it takes the boldness to rise up in your inner man and say, "Father, I made a mistake, and I ask you by the blood of Jesus to forgive me. I'm sincere in my heart, I want your forgiveness. Devil, you take a hike. Jesus paid for my sin, and it's none of your business." Then, you just go on and be happy, be joyful. But you are probably thinking, "I keep doing the same stupid thing over and over and over." I used to think that, too, until I stopped being condemned about it. *When you stop being condemned about what you have done, you will stop doing it.*

Guilt and condemnation keep you weighed down and depressed to the point that you can't be free. It takes a bold person not to be condemned. You have to be bold and operate in faith and rise up and *say no to guilt*. The devil will tell you, "Do you mean you're not even going to feel bad about that? Why, you ought to at least feel bad for a few hours. That was really a bad thing you did." All you say is, "No, I'm sure not. I'm not going to feel bad about it at all." The first few times are tough, but it only takes three or four times, and you get the hang of it.

In Isaiah 53, verses 5,6 and 11 in the *Amplified Bible* it tells us that when Jesus took our sins for us that He also bore the guilt (and that includes condemnation). The devil doesn't want you to be free from condemnation. Why? Because if you are condemned, you can't really bask in the love of God. Condemnation separates you from God and comes down between you and God like a steel wall. You can't see Father God when you are standing in guilt. All you can see is the guilt and the sin in front of you.

Walk free of condemnation and believe that when God said His grace was sufficient to cover even your sin, He meant it. He loves you, and His grace and forgiveness are free gifts. Receive them today!

God loves *you*!

3

. . . .

Love Is Relationship

"And we know (understand, recognize, are conscious of, by observation and by experience) and believe (adhere to and put faith in and rely on) the love God cherishes for us. God is love, and he who dwells and continues in love dwells and continues in God, and God dwells and continues in him."

1 John 4:16 AMP

How can you be more conscious and aware of God's love? No matter how much He loves you, if you are not conscious and aware of it, it is not going to do you any good. You know how good it makes you feel if somebody really shows you a lot of love? You feel so warm and wonderful that you could just take the world by the tail because you know somebody loves you. God loves you, and He wants to show you that love. He wants you to spend time with Him on a daily basis.

Do you have a real personal relationship with God? Just because you got saved a long time ago does not mean you are enjoying a rich fellowship with God. When I open my eyes in the morning, the first thing I think about is God, and He is the last thing I think about before I go to bed at night. And I think about God all day in between. There is nothing that I want any more in this whole, wide world than to serve my God and to please Him. And that's worth anything that you have to lay down to get it.

There is a God-shaped hole inside of us that only God can fill. Nothing else you can run after or desire can fill that place. You may say to yourself, "I know that already, I received Jesus." But are you receiving Him every minute, every day, in every situation? Are you receiving the love of God?

God loves you, and you are special to Him. He created us to fellowship with Him. This is His greatest desire and His perfect will for your life. He leans over the throne every morning and says, "Good morning, I love you."

A friend of mine had a vision once while she was praying. She saw the Father go into the homes of the people of America when they got up in the morning. He went in all ready to fellowship and talk to them. He got Himself a chair at the table and sat down. The people got up, and they came, and they went; they came, and they went. They kept telling God, "Later. Stay right there for just a little while, God. As soon as I get this done, I'm going to talk to You. I'm going to fellowship with You later, God. Later, God. Later, God."

The end of the day came, and the girl who saw this said it broke her heart because she saw God, with slumped over shoulders, leave the home. And nobody had ever come to talk to Him that day.

Don't get too busy. If you don't have time to pray and spend time with God, then you are too busy. Take the time to tell God how much you love Him. When everything else passes away and it is all over but the shouting, there is nothing but God. That's it. And if you don't have a relationship with

Him then, it is going to be a little late to start getting to that point. That doesn't mean you will not go to heaven, but you have missed the joy of living a victorious life.

I suggest you set aside a year, and just *let God love you*. Stop trying in your own power to operate in faith and be God's man or woman of faith and power. Just back off and act like a little child. You just crawl up in your Father's lap, and let God love you. You can't love Him back until you let Him love you.

First John 4:16 AMP says,

"And we know (understand, recognize, are conscious of, by observation and by experience) and believe (adhere to and put faith in and rely on) the love God cherishes for us...."

Did you get up this morning and spend some time thinking about how much God loves you? When you first get up in the morning, you don't usually feel like doing anything. But you need to use your mouth to activate your flesh and allow your spirit man to rise up and do all kinds of wonderful things.

So when you get up in the morning, you need to begin to say, "Oh, Father, I thank You that You love me so much. I thank You that You sent Jesus to die for me. Oh, Father, I thank You that I'm with the Holy Ghost. I thank You that the resurrection power abides on the inside of me. Oh, Lord, I thank You that everywhere I go today I'm a blessing. *God, You love **me**. You love me*, right here in my little house. *You love **me**!* I'm Your special child. I'm the apple of Your eye. You love me!"

You have to talk to yourself and get yourself *aware* and *conscious* that you are surrounded and drowned in the love of God. The Bible says that God has a picture of you tattooed on the palms of His hands. (Isa. 49:16 AMP.) I can just see Him up there saying, "Look, see that? Oh, isn't she beautiful? I just love her so much. Just look at My kids, right there in the palms of My hands." He has *you* there as a constant reminder that He loves you and longs to fellowship with you.

Remember to be thankful before God and develop a relationship of fellowship. Sometimes you need to fall down on your face in prayer and just thank God that you are saved. Back off and love God. Read on in 1 John 4:16,17 AMP where He says,

"...God is love, and he who dwells and continues in love dwells and continues in God, and God dwells and continues in him.

"In this [union and communion with Him] love is brought to completion and attains perfection with us, that we may have confidence for the day of judgment."

Knowing that God loves you gives you confidence in Him and trust in His faithfulness.

All blessings will come through letting God love you: greater faith, victory over sin, healing, prosperity and joy. It has to come by allowing God to love you. A lot of times we turn that around and think, "Well, I've got to love God." I believe first you have to let God love you. I don't believe you can express your love to God until you let God love you.

I can tell you to fellowship with God and that you really need to fellowship with God, but how do you do that? When God told me to fellowship with Him, I just got on my couch and sat down and said, "Now what, God?" That's right! I didn't know how to fellowship with God because, still at that point, I really didn't know how much God loved me.

How can you express your feelings to people, really just love them and adore them, if you are not sure they love you? You would be afraid of making a fool out of yourself. You are comfortable with those you know will love and receive you. I can say things and do things with my husband that I couldn't do with anybody else because I know that he loves me. It is the same way with God.

So step out and make a start. Give God an opportunity, and He will teach you how to fellowship with Him. Ask yourself this question right now: *Am I comfortable with God?*

God loves *you*!

4

....

Love, Trust
and Faith

"For [if we are] in Christ Jesus, neither circumcision nor uncircumcision counts for anything, but only faith activated and energized and expressed and working through love."

Galatians 5:6 AMP

Most of us spend a lot of time trying to have faith. We know that without faith it is impossible to please God (Heb. 11:6), so we work and strive at having more faith. But faith is of the heart, and you get it only through a relationship of loving fellowship with God. I can't really teach you faith, but I can teach you the principles of faith and make you so hungry for it you will do anything to get it. It only comes by revelation from God.

Stop trying so hard to get faith and please God, and start spending all that time and effort with God, loving Him. Just go around all day loving Him and letting Him love you.

"For we walk by faith [we regulate our lives and conduct ourselves by our conviction or belief respecting man's relationship to God and divine things, with trust and holy fervor; thus we walk] not by sight or appearance."

2 Corinthians 5:7 AMP

Once when I was reading that Scripture, God started speaking some dynamic things to my heart. I am trying to walk by faith. In every single thing in my life, I want to walk by faith. And the *Amplified Bible* says in 2 Corinthians 5:7 that "...we regulate our lives and conduct ourselves by our conviction or belief respecting man's relationship to God."

In other words, *I am only going to be able to walk in faith based on what I believe about my relationship with God.* Do you understand that? A person who believes he is unrighteous might as well forget walking in faith. A person who believes he is an old worm in the dust and God does not love Him might as well forget the faith walk, too. A lot of people are trying to walk in faith, but they don't have these other things in their hearts.

Galatians 5:6 says, faith works by love. God put this in my heart: "Everybody thinks that this Scripture means that if they don't love other people, their faith won't work. That isn't what it means at all. What it really means is if they don't know how much I love them, their faith won't work." Faith will not work without love. But it isn't your ability to love other people. It is your letting God Almighty love you.

There is a big difference in that. Trusting God and walking in faith is leaning on Him and trusting Him for everything. You can't do that with someone if you don't know he loves you. You might as well forget it. You are never going to be able to trust God if you don't know He loves you.

If you really knew how much God loves you, you would have less trouble receiving a healing. You would have less trouble receiving your financial needs met.

The reason you can't receive is that you don't really believe, totally, that God is giving it to you. You might say, "I want to believe that, but how do I believe that?"

You have the love of God inside you, and all you need is to begin to recognize it when He shows you. The Bible says, "We love Him, because He first loved us" (1 John 4:19). It would be impossible for you to love God if you weren't assured of the fact that He loved you first.

It is all down inside you, in your heart. It is in there! *God loves you! You are wonderful! You are beautiful! You are precious! You are tremendous! God loves you!* Nobody in all the world will ever love you like God loves you.

You don't *need* anybody but God, but He will give you other people in your life. The truth is that if there were nobody but you and God, you would get by fine. God will be your best friend. He will be your mate if you don't have one. He will be your mother or father if you don't have one.

God loves you that much. That's how you can believe Him for anything. He loves you so much that you know He wants you to have it. And until you know that God wants you to have it, you are never going to be operating in enough faith to receive anything.

Faith works by letting God love you. It doesn't work by your ability to go out and love somebody else. Let God love you and go around all day just telling God, "Oh, God, I know You love me. Hallelujah! Father, I praise You. I magnify Your name."

Smith Wigglesworth was a great apostle of God. Someone asked him if he had long seasons in prayer, and he said, "I rarely ever pray more than 30 minutes, but I rarely ever go 30 minutes without praying." He said once that if he went more than fifteen minutes at one time without having some communication with God, he had to repent.

We are trying to get things from the wrong end. You can't make it happen by your works. God will bless you because He loves you. He will give to you the same way He gave you your salvation.

You are not going to get a family member, or anyone else, saved by working at it. Let God love you. Then, by the time you see the family member, you will be ready to love him. The Bible tells you that if you will love them and stop trying to win them with your words and all your fancy ways, you will draw them to Jesus. The Spirit of God will draw your family through His love. But you can't love others if you don't let God love you first.

Ephesians 2:8 AMP says, "For it is by free grace (God's unmerited favor) that you are saved...." Do you realize that you did nothing to get saved? Most of us were just as rotten as the day is long when Jesus saved us, and it certainly was not based on our good works or our ability to do anything right. It was because of only one thing: God loved us so much that he gave His only begotten Son that whosoever believed in Him would not perish but have everlasting life. (John 3:16.)

Grace can also be defined as God's willingness to use His ability in your life to meet all your needs. Just as God, by grace, gave you enough faith to get saved, He also, because of His love, gives you the faith to believe He is your healer. He gives you the faith to believe He is your provider.

If the faith He imparted to you for your salvation was enough to save you from all your sins, that same faith is on the inside of you to meet all the rest of your needs all your life. If you believe that God loves you, and really begin to know it, then you will begin to really trust Him. You will be convicted of the truthfulness of God's Word. You will *know* that He would never lie to you because He loves you.

According to the *Amplified Bible*, "faith" is "the leaning of your entire human personality on Him" [God] "in absolute trust and confidence in His power, wisdom, and goodness" (Col. 1:4). As you allow God to love you, you will learn to love Him and trust Him, and you *will* have faith.

God loves *you*!

5

. . . .

Freedom From Fear

"There is no fear in love [dread does not exist], but full-grown (complete, perfect) love turns fear out of doors and expels every trace of terror! For fear brings with it the thought of punishment, and [so] he who is afraid has not reached the full maturity of love [is not yet grown into love's complete perfection]."

1 John 4:18 AMP

We usually go along just fine in faith, confident that God loves us, trusting Him. Then all of a sudden, something attacks us.

The big stealer of faith is circumstances — those bad things that happen to us. You don't have much trouble believing God loves you until the circumstances make it look like He doesn't.

Then the devil comes in with fear and condemnation to separate you from the very thing that will set you free – God's love. "Well, what about this?" he says. "I thought God loved you. So why are bad things happening to you? You must have done something awful. God is really mad at you."

Then you lose your confidence before God, and He can't help you if you are not confident. You can't be confident, or full of faith, if you don't know that God loves you. And if you receive the devil's load of fear and condemnation, you don't know how much God loves you.

First John 4:18 says a tremendously powerful thing "...perfect love casteth out fear." I meditated and meditated on that Scripture, trying to figure it out, and one day God finally dropped it in my spirit. Perfect love casts out fear, and God *is* that perfect love. And when you know how perfect that love is toward you, there is nothing in all of creation that you can be afraid of. It is impossible to be afraid if you have a personal revelation that God loves you.

It is impossible to fear failure if you know that God loves you. You can't fail if you are dependent on God. The only way you are going to fail is if you are dependent on yourself. If you know that God loves you, you will not fear failure. If you know that God loves you, you will not fear rejection.

God's love is of such magnitude that it covers everything. Do you think that the same God that saved you and set you free is going to condemn you? Satan is the condemner. God will convict you of sin in your life, and He will show you the way out. The devil will condemn you and tell you there is no way out.

In the *Amplified Bible* this Scripture reads:

"There is no fear in love [dread does not exist], but full-grown (complete, perfect) love turns fear out of doors and expels every trace of terror! For fear brings with it the thought of punishment, and [so] he who is afraid has not reached the full maturity of love [is not yet grown into love's complete perfection]."

1 John 4:18

A lot of people think that Scripture means that if you can love me enough, then you will not be afraid of me, or if you can love somebody enough, then fear will leave your life. But that isn't what it means.

It means if you let God love you, then you will not be afraid. You have to let God love you if you don't want to have fear in your life. *Receive God's love for you right now by an act of faith.* Go ahead. Reach out in faith and take all of God's love for you.

Right after God gave me this revelation on His love casting out fear, I had to put it into practice. We had been having car trouble, and we thought the transmission was going out in our car, and we have a big transmission! It would probably have cost four or five hundred dollars to replace it if it was completely out, and we didn't have the money. So we just kept driving it.

God ministered to me that morning and said, "Joyce, just go around all day loving Me, and let Me love you. You don't have to do anything else. You don't have to be a woman of great faith. All you have to do is go around loving Me and letting Me love you. Just all the time. Let Me love you."

So, I was going around building myself up in my most holy faith and was singing, making up songs to God and having a wonderful time. Then all of a sudden, I heard my husband back in the garage. But he had gone to work about 45 minutes before! He opened the door and said, "I never could get the car out of first gear. We are going to have to take it in."

I just shut the door and started laughing. It was not something I decided to do. It just came out. It just rose up out of my spirit, and God showed me that it was because I had been letting Him love me all morning that I was able to laugh. Letting God love you opens the door for faith to come out of you. I just began to laugh, and that was faith.

Abraham laughed the laugh of faith. When God came to him and told him he was going to have a son, Abraham backed off and laughed, saying, "Glory! I believe it." Now Sarah laughed the laugh of doubt and unbelief, and God corrected her, but He didn't jump onto Abraham. He didn't call

Abraham down for laughing because there is a laugh of faith.

When the devil comes against you and what he is trying to do seems so foolish and so ridiculous, and you know your God so well that it doesn't scare you, you laugh in faith. You know that God loves you, and He has it covered.

So as I was laughing about my transmission, God spoke something to my heart in a still, small voice, but it was very powerful. He said to me three times, "If you operate like this with Me, Joyce, I'll never disappoint you." It was like it just came through the atmosphere of my house. "I'll never disappoint you. I'll never disappoint you."

If you will lean on God and let God love you and you love Him, you can forget all the work of trying to operate in faith. You just let God love you, and you love Him, and He will bring it to pass. The love of God will rise up inside of you and cast out all the fear.

God loves *you*!

6

....

Love Reaches Out

"And this command (charge, order, injunction) we have from Him: that he who loves God shall love his brother [believer] also."

1 John 4:21

You are God's special child. He told you that in Deuteronomy 7:6. If you will start to act that way, it will begin to change the world. You will go into the supermarket with a smile on your face and grab your grocery cart and say, "Everything that I touch is blessed. Hallelujah! They're blessed to have me in this store today. Glory!" Just go whistling through the store, singing, being special wherever you go.

When we begin to know how special we are and start acting like God loves us, we can win the world for Jesus. Love will spread like wildfire. But it is not going to do any good to go around saying you are a Christian, then growling at everyone. You say, "I'm a Christian – I'm a Christian," but when a car cuts in front of you, you say, "Come on, dummy, get out of my way. Don't you know I've got to get to church? I'm going to be late for the meeting, you nut."

That's the kind of stuff we do sometimes. Are you ready to grab hold of victory? Just reach out there in the spirit, and grab hold of victory and say, "Devil, you have led me around with lies and fear long enough. I am a special person, and I am going to have victory in the name of Jesus because God loves me, devil, and there is nothing you can do about it!"

God's love inside of you will set you free from fear, and you will not be afraid to reach out to others with love. God wants you to believe it when He says He will do greater works through you because Jesus went to His Father. Do you really believe God will use you? God will give you what you believe Him for. You can't be afraid to step out.

I couldn't even begin to tell you how many times I have stood on the edge of a faith cliff, right on the edge of doing something scary, and God said, "Come on, Joyce, come on. I'll do great things through you. Come on." And I just jumped right out in the middle of it, and God has never let me down one time.

Do you know why I don't have to worry about stepping out and being a failure? Because I know God loves me. He loves me, and He knows I love Him, and through His grace I have laid down my life for Him. If you have done that, and you love God, and He loves you, then nothing in all creation can be a problem to you that can't be overcome.

"Who shall ever separate us from Christ's love? Shall suffering and affliction and tribulation? Or calamity and distress? Or persecution or hunger or destitution or peril or sword?

"Even as it is written, For Thy sake we are put to death all the day long; we are regarded and counted as sheep for the slaughter.

"Yet amid all these things we are more

than conquerors and gain a surpassing victory through Him Who loved us.

"For I am persuaded beyond doubt (am sure) that neither death nor life, nor angels nor principalities, nor things impending and threatening, nor things to come, nor powers,

"Nor height nor depth, nor anything else in all creation will be able to separate us from the love of God which is in Christ Jesus our Lord."

Romans 8:35-39

You may have no conception of how much God wants you to be free. God hurts when you are unhappy. Sometimes you get up and you are in a bad mood all day. Do you know the kind of day I am talking about? You are kicking the cat, yelling at the kids, hating the neighbors, and you have this old grumpy, grouchy look on your face. "All I ever do is work, work, work, and nobody appreciates it."

I know how you act because I have

done that, too. When the kids come home, you think, *Why don't you stay at school fourteen hours a day instead of seven?"*

Do you know that hurts God? I am not trying to make you feel bad. I am trying to get you to realize that if you can believe God loves you, you are going to begin to respond to that love, then that love will fill you up and start pouring out all over everybody else. You will be free to be a sweetheart, flowing in the fruit of kindness.

If you will grab hold of the fact that God loves you, your healing will come forth, your prosperity will come forth and your needs will be met. Why? *You will just start to relax.*

The main reason God can't give us most of the things He wants to give us is that we are so busy trying to get them that He can't catch us long enough to put them on us. God wants you to rest in Him and just love Him. He wants you to let Him love you and just receive.

The devil can't stop the flow if you are a lover because if you are a lover, you are going to be a giver. You can't love and not give.

The last part of the Scripture in Deuteronomy 7:6 AMP says, "...God has chosen you to be a special people." God has called you. Right now your main job might be in your home with your family, but God has called you. If you really want to be used by God, you can be used by God. But you have to get this foundation laid first. *You have to know that God loves you.*

Don't expend all of your spiritual energy concentrating on yourself and getting your needs met. Tell God what you want simply and quickly then develop your faith to meet the needs of other people. Jesus would pray and seek the face of His Father in order to get built up to go out and meet the needs of all those people who went to his faith seminars.

Then He would preach the Word to them, lay hands on them, and they would receive miracles. He was not sitting off in the corner somewhere all the time trying to believe God for things that He wanted. You need to tell God what you want, but it just needs to be a matter of fact thing. The main desire of your life, though, should be to meet the needs of other people.

True prosperity, accurately defined, is the ability to use God's ability to meet every need that comes before you. The love of God will give you the ability to put the needs of others first. Do you think God loves you enough to make you able to reach out and love those who are not too much fun to love – the grouchy, unappreciative ones?

It doesn't take anything to love somebody who loves you. There is no trick to that. Any old sinner can do that. But when you love the unlovable, you press in and keep loving them, and you keep loving them, and you *keep loving them*. Then the love of God will change them.

It may take a year. It may take five years. It may take twenty-five years, but it is worth it. *How long did Jesus wait for you?*

God loves you, and He loves all those

people all around you, too. Saved or sinner, He loves them, and He wants to use you as a channel to pour out His love.

Don't be afraid to step out. God's love is setting you free from fear and condemnation, and He has given you the ability to love. Be determined to spread God's love around. Start just being friendly with people. Make it your business to be friendly and be a blessing to people in the Body of Christ.

Ask people over for dinner and have people come and visit you. Shake hands with people, *smile*. God has something for you to do. He wants to use you in ways that He can't use any other creature on this earth.

There are people that only you could minister to. Nobody else could reach that person, but *you*. Ask God to show you ways to reach out with His love, and He will teach you.

God loves *you*!

7

···

God's Love Will Change You

"In this is love: not that we loved God, but that He loved us and sent His Son to be the propitiation (the atoning sacrifice) for our sins."

1 John 4:10

God loves us, but I don't think many of us actually comprehend the love that God loves us with. God has shown me, through the study I have done on this, that if we really knew in our spirits how much God loved us, we would rise up and be a lot different than what we are a lot of the time.

Meditate on God's love for you. That's what is going to change you. If you don't like something about yourself, *"knowing that you know"* that God loves you is going to change it.

How does it make you feel when you know that somebody loves you? It makes you feel good, right? Do you feel ugly? God told me that some of the people who would be reading this book hate themselves. You hate the things you do, and you have not accepted that you are a new creation – you are constantly fighting the old nature.

As long as you go around feeling badly about yourself all the time, not liking yourself, hating yourself, not realizing how special you are, you are never going to act special. The Bible says, "For as he thinks in his heart, so is he" (Prov. 23:7 AMP). It is all because you have not really grabbed hold of the fact that *God loves you*. It is a powerful thing to know how much He loves *you*.

God wants you to get with Him yourself on a daily basis. That's what will change you. If you don't put God first, you are putting Him in a position where He can't do for you what He wants to do. It is the private time you spend with God, just loving Him and letting Him love you, that's going to cause you to grow up and be strong in your spirit man.

The biggest majority of people are lazy, and they would rather not do that. They would like it much better if somebody would do it for them. *Don't make excuses.* Everyone reading this who is not fellowshipping with God and is being convicted because of what I am writing is going to have the devil coming in right behind that conviction and saying, "But you've got all these other things to do."

I know how it goes – the devil gives you one excuse after another. Get serious with God, and cry out to Him. *The Word of God and fellowship with Him will change you.* God has made you able. Paul says in Philippians 4:13, "I can do all things through Christ which strengtheneth me." In other words, there is nothing in all creation you can't do through the power of Jesus Christ.

As fast as God points out a problem to you, you ought to rise up in power and victory and knock it off. If you will rise up and receive God's love for you and refuse to let that dirty, lying devil tell you how rotten and no good you are, you will start acting victoriously.

You may be acting awful now, but you can act differently if you will believe that you are a new creation on the inside. You will never change or act one bit differently until you begin to rise up and say, "Praise God, I'm special. I'm holy. God chose me. He has purified me by the Blood of the Lamb. I'm going to act that way. And I don't care, devil, how many mistakes I make. God's big enough to pick me up and cause me to go on. *He cleans up my messes!*"

What problems can defeat you if you "know that you know" that God loves you? There aren't any. You will be victorious in them all.

Would you like to be an overcomer? Answer this then – do you want to have something to overcome? That's the only way you are going to grow up. If you never have any problems and you never have anything to overcome, what are you going to cut your faith teeth on?

Use the problems that come against you as opportunities to grow. Find out what God will do because He loves you! If you will lean on God and let God love you and you love Him, you can forget all the *trying* to operate in faith and enter into rest.

If you just let God love you and you love Him, then you will go around like some drunk person all the time – drunk in the spirit. That's when the circumstances in your life will not get to you because you are just going around operating in the love of God.

When I was baptized in the Holy Spirit, for the first three weeks it was like I was drunk with God's love. People kept saying to me, "What is wrong with you? You are so different. I can't believe it, Joyce. What has happened to you?" These people came to me three weeks later and said, "What has happened to your life?"

I didn't have to say one thing to convince them I had changed. They could see it. If you operate in the love of God, you are going to be smiling all the time. You are going to be beautiful. You are going to have energy and strength. You are going to be able to minister to people because you will be so charged up in the Holy Ghost all the time that any need you have is going to be met.

Say to yourself, "*God loves me*. Hallelujah, *God loves me*. I'm His special child. *God loves me!*" Now go ahead – take a big leap of faith and believe it.

God really does love *you*!

Experience
A New Life

If you have never invited Jesus to be your Lord and Savior, I invite you to do so now. You can pray this prayer, and if you are really sincere about it, you will experience a new life in Christ.

Father God, I believe Jesus Christ is Your Son, the Savior of the world. I believe He died on the cross for me, and He bore all of my sins. He paid the price for my sins. He took the punishment I deserved. I believe Jesus was resurrected from the dead and is now seated at Your right hand. I need You, Jesus. Forgive my sins, save me, come to live inside me. I want to be born again.

Now believe Jesus is living in your heart. You are forgiven, made righteous, and you will go to heaven.

Find a good church that's teaching God's Word and begin to grow in Christ. Nothing will change in your life without knowledge of God's Word. John 8:31-32 AMP says, "If ye continue in my word, then are ye my disciples indeed. And ye shall know the truth, and the truth shall make you free."

I exhort you to take hold of God's Word, plant it deep in your heart, and according to 2 Corinthians 3:18, as you look into the Word, you will be transformed into the image of Jesus Christ.

Write and let me know you have accepted Jesus, and ask for a free booklet on how to begin your new life in Christ.

With Love,
Joyce

About the Author

Joyce Meyer has been teaching the Word of God since 1976 and in full-time ministry since 1980. As an associate pastor at Life Christian Center in St. Louis, Missouri, she developed, coordinated and taught a weekly meeting known as "Life In The Word." After more than five years, the Lord brought it to a conclusion, directing her to establish her own ministry and call it "Life In The Word, Inc."

Joyce's "Life In The Word" radio broadcast is heard on over 250 stations nationwide. Joyce's 30-minute "Life In The Word With Joyce Meyer" television program was released in 1993 and is broadcast throughout the United States and several foreign countries. Her teaching tapes are enjoyed internationally.

She travels extensively conducting Life In The Word conferences, as well as speaking in local churches.

Joyce and her husband, Dave, business administrator at Life In The Word, have been married for 30 years and are the parents of four children. Three are married, and their youngest son resides with them in Fenton, Missouri, a St. Louis suburb.

Joyce believes the call on her life is to establish believers in God's Word. She says, "Jesus died to set the captives free, and far too many Christians have little or no victory in their daily lives." Finding herself in the same situation many years ago, and having found freedom to live in victory through applying God's Word, Joyce goes equipped to set captives free and to exchange *ashes for beauty*.

Joyce has taught on emotional healing and related subjects in meetings all over the country, helping multiplied thousands. She has recorded over 150 different audio cassette albums and is the author of 16 books to help the Body of Christ on various topics.

Her "Emotional Healing Package" contains over 23 hours of teaching on the subject. Albums included in this package are: "Confidence"; "Beauty for Ashes" (includes a syllabus); "Managing Your Emotions"; "Bitterness, Resentment, and Unforgiveness"; "Root of Rejection"; and a 90-minute Scripture/music tape entitled, "Healing the Brokenhearted."

Joyce's "Mind Package" features five different audio tape series on the subject of the mind. They include: "Mental Strongholds and Mindsets"; "Wilderness Mentality"; "The Mind of the Flesh"; "The Wandering, Wondering Mind"; and "Mind, Mouth, Moods & Attitudes." The package also contains Joyce's powerful 260-page book, *Battlefield of the Mind*.

On the subject of love she has two tape series entitled "Love Is..." and "Love: The Ultimate Power."

Write to Joyce Meyer's office for a resource catalog and further information on how to obtain the tapes you need to bring total healing to your life.

To contact the author, write:

Joyce Meyer
Life In The Word, Inc.
P. O. Box 655
Fenton, Missouri 63026
or call:
(314) 349-0303

*Please include your testimony
or help received from this
book when you write.*

Your prayer requests are welcome.

In Canada, please write:
Joyce Meyer Ministries Canada, Inc.
P. O. Box 2995
London, Ontario N6A 4H9

In Australia, please write:
Joyce Meyer Ministries-Australia
Locked Bag 77
Mansfield Delivery Centre
Queensland 4122
or call:
(07) 3349 1200

Books by Joyce Meyer

Prepare to Prosper
Me and My Big Mouth
Healing the Brokenhearted
Do It Afraid!
Expect a Move of God in Your Life...Suddenly!
*Enjoying Where You Are On the Way
to Where You Are Going*
The Most Important Decision You'll Ever Make
When, God, When?
Why, God, Why?
The Word, the Name, the Blood
Battlefield of the Mind
"Tell Them I Love Them"
Peace
The Root of Rejection
Beauty for Ashes
If Not for the Grace of God

By Dave Meyer
Nuggets of Life

Available from your local bookstore.

Harrison House
Tulsa, Oklahoma 74153

For additional copies
of this book
in Canada contact:
Word Alive • P. O. Box 670
Niverville, Manitoba • CANADA R0A 1E0

For additional copies
of this book
in Canada contact:

Word Alive
P. O. Box 670
Niverville, Manitoba
CANADA R0A 1E0

The Harrison House Vision

Proclaiming the truth and the power
Of the Gospel of Jesus Christ
With excellence;

Challenging Christians to
Live victoriously,
Grow spiritually,
Know God intimately.